CU00240635

DEVELOPING RESILIENCE

A WORKBOOK FOR TEENS

STACY ZEIGER

BUILDING KIDS' CHARACTER

Resilience (*n.*) – the ability to adapt and recover from adversity or incidences of change that arise in life.

Synonyms: flexibility, elasticity, endurance

Related words: strength, courage, fortitude, stamina, backbone

Table of Contents

What Is Resilience?

Have you ever faced a situation that has been hard on you physically, mentally and/or emotionally? It may be something small, such as missing the game-winning shot, failing a class or getting injured and not being able to play a sport anymore. It may be something bigger, such as dealing with your parents' divorce, losing someone close to you or regularly being bullied or harassed.

Resilience is the ability to bounce back from these types of situations. Instead of letting something drag you down, you use it to become a stronger, more focused person.

Resilience in Your Life

Stop and think about your own life. Have you faced any major changes? Any major misfortunes? Any situations that have caused you a lot of stress? Take a moment and write down some of the challenges that you've had to face or that you're currently facing.

Now look at that list of challenges and think about how you've handled or are currently handling them. Are stress and frustration getting the best of you? Are you getting down on yourself? Write down your responses, good or bad, to those challenges.

> *"If you voluntarily quit in the face of adversity,*
> *you'll wonder about it for the rest of your life."*
>
> – Former President Bill Clinton

Read the quote from former President Bill Clinton again. What do you think it means?

Being resilient requires standing up to any adversity that you face and continuing to run the race of life.

> *"I have missed more than 9,000 shots in my career. I have lost almost 300 games.*
> *On 26 occasions I have been entrusted to take the game-winning shot... and I*
> *missed. I have failed over and over and over again in my life. And that's precisely*
> *why I succeed."*
>
> - Michael Jordan

Think about what you already know about resilience. How does the quote above show Michael Jordan's resilience?

> *"That which does not destroy,*
> *strengthens."*
>
> - Fredrich Nietzsche

The quote from Nietzsche may remind you of a more modern saying, "what doesn't kill you only makes you stronger." Do you think Nietzsche's quote and the more modern saying are true?

> *"The strongest oak of the forest is not the one that is protected from the storm and hidden from the sun. It's the one that stands in the open where it is compelled to struggle for its existence against the winds and rains and the scorching sun."*
>
> - Napoleon Hill

One of the best places to learn about resilience is in nature. While some human activities have an effect on the resilience of nature, nature is generally fairly resilient when it comes to facing adversity.

Think of the small trees sprouting from the ground after a forest is destroyed in a fire.

Think of trees that fall but continue to grow new branches and leaves in different positions.

Think about the flowers that grow in the cracks of the sidewalk, the weeds that you're constantly pulling up from the garden but that always reappear and the dandelions that may cover your yard in the summer.

> "The bamboo that bends is stronger than the oak that resists."
>
> - Japanese Proverb

Think about the Japanese proverb and the pictures of nature. What can nature teach you about being resilient or bouncing back in the face of adversity?

Why It's Important to Be Resilient

Sometimes it's hard to be resilient. You may feel like your life is over or that there is no way out. You may be embarrassed by your situation or feel like no one will understand your problems and emotions. When you're at the bottom (or feel like you are), you have two choices: stay at the bottom or get back up.

> *"Inside of a ring or out, ain't nothing wrong with going down. It's staying down that's wrong."*
>
> - Muhammad Ali

Chances are you've seen at least one inspirational sports movie in your life. You know the type – the football player looks like he'll never make it into a game, the horse breaks a leg and will never race again, the boxer is knocked down and rises at the last second. Imagine how different movies like *Rudy, Seabiscuit, Cinderella Man, Rocky, Miracle, We Are Marshall* and *Pride* would be if the main characters were not resilient.

Think About It

A boxer is in the ring. He has reached the 12th round of a title fight. His opponent knocks him down. The referee starts counting to ten. The boxer is in some pain, but he could easily get back up. He has a choice to make: stay down and end the round or get back up and potentially win the fight. Answer the questions in the boxes below, being sure to consider the future consequences of the boxer's decision (future fights, career, what people think of him, etc.).

What happens if the boxer stays down?	What happens if the boxer gets back up?

Celebrity Spotlight: Jennifer Hudson

In 2004, Jennifer Hudson was on *American Idol*. Even though she didn't win, her star began to rise. She had a starring role in the movie *Dreamgirls*, and her music career was taking off. Hudson was on top, and it seemed like nothing could bring her down. But in 2008, Hudson's mother, brother and nephew were murdered. After this tragedy, her focus changed.

Hudson spent a few months out of the spotlight while she dealt with the grief over losing her family members, but when she came back, she came back big. In February 2009, Hudson poured her grief and emotions into a performance of *The Star-Spangled Banner* at the Super Bowl. After that day, she continued to devote her energy to her career and herself. Hudson has created hit albums and, famously, lost 80 pounds with the help of Weight Watchers.

While she still grieves, Hudson has proved that nothing is going to stop her from living out her dream.

A few words of wisdom from Jennifer Hudson:

- *In a recent interview, I was asked how I reconciled being a Christian with performing at events for my gay fans. I find it upsetting that some folks equate being a Christian with being intolerant of gay people. That may, unfortunately, be true for some, but it is not true for me. I have talked often of my love and support of the gay community. I have said again and again that it was the gay community that supported me long before and long after American Idol, and kept me working and motivated. It is the gay community that celebrated my voice and my size and my personality long before Dreamgirls. Yes, I was raised Baptist. Yes, I was taught that the Bible has certain views on homosexuality. The Bible also teaches us not to judge. It teaches us to love one another as God loves us all. I love my sister, my two best friends and my director dearly. They happen to be gay. So what? While some search for controversy, I hope that my friends and fans who know me know where I stand.*

- *"I never thought that I was overweight. I thought my old look was pretty normal. That was how all the girls looked growing up in Chicago... I loved that I stood out in a room. You knew when you saw this woman, it was Jennifer Hudson."*

Who Are You?

In order to be resilient, you have to know who you are. How do you define yourself? Are you the teen who isn't very smart, the girl who barely speaks English, the boy without a father, the teen without a home, the girl who isn't very pretty or the boy who is gay and harassed on a daily basis? While negative situations and traits are a part of your life, they do not have to define you. Neither do the opinions of others.

> "No one can make you feel inferior without your consent."
>
> - Eleanor Roosevelt

Being resilient requires knowing who you are and having a positive opinion of yourself. Words that describe a resilient person include: strong, tough, unsinkable, determined, optimistic, responsible.

Do these words describe you? If not, what changes can you make so they describe you better? Take a second and think of ways these words/traits are displayed in your life or how you could display them.

1. I am (can be) strong when....

2. I am (can be) tough when...

3. I am (can be) unsinkable because...

4. I am (can be) determined to...

5. I am (can be) optimistic about...

6. I am (can be) responsible for...

Now it's time to explore yourself a little more.

Describe yourself in a short paragraph.

If there's anything negative in the paragraph, cross it out.

Let's think about your positive traits a little more...

1. What are three positive adjectives that describe you?

2. A special committee has decided to honor you for something great. What award will you receive?

3. How would the people who are closest to you and like you best describe you?

If you had trouble answering these questions, you should take some time to discover the positives inside of you. Some ways to do this include:

1. Challenge yourself to look in the mirror and spend a minute telling yourself how great you are.
2. Make a list of the things that you like about yourself.
3. Ask the people close to you what they like about you.
4. Find a few pictures of yourself and tape positive adjectives to them. Glue them in a notebook or hang them on your mirror or beside your bed.

Celebrity Spotlight: Ellen DeGeneres

If you've ever watched *The Ellen DeGeneres Show*, you probably can't imagine Ellen DeGeneres ever going through a rough time. Sometimes, however, comedians hide their struggles in their humor. In 1997, DeGeneres decided to come out on her hit sitcom *Ellen*. She got a lot of praise for coming out, won an Emmy for the show and was named one of the most fascinating people of the year.

Having an openly gay character on national TV was a big deal in 1997, and DeGeneres faced a lot of backlash for her decision to come out. Bomb threats were sent to her studio. Advertisers dropped out of the show and, for a few years, she had trouble finding people who were willing to work with her. Famous people called her names and shared negative opinions of her all over the media.

Obviously, DeGeneres overcame the backlash and the struggles, but how did she do it? DeGeneres regularly shares in interviews how coming out was a freeing experience for her. Even though it was hard, it was something she had to do for herself. From there, she focused on living her life and dedicated herself to what she enjoyed the most – making people laugh.

A few words of wisdom from Ellen DeGeneres:

- "When you take risks, you learn that there will be times when you succeed and there will be times when you fail, and both are equally important."

- "True beauty is not related to what color your hair is or what color your eyes are. True beauty is about who you are as a human being, your principles, your moral compass."

- "For me, it's that I contributed … that I'm on this planet doing some good and making people happy. That's to me the most important thing, that my hour of television is positive and upbeat and an antidote for all the negative stuff going on in life."

- "When I was younger, I thought success was something different. I thought, 'When I grow up, I want to be famous. I want to be a star. I want to be in movies. When I grow up, I want to see the world, drive nice cars. I want to have groupies.' But my idea of success is different today. For me, the most important thing in your life is to live your life with integrity and not to give into peer pressure, to try to be something that you're not. To live your life as an honest and compassionate person. To contribute in some way."

Strengths and Weaknesses

Knowing your strengths and weaknesses can help you develop resilience. When you know what you're good at, you can use it to your advantage. When you know where you are weak, you can build up that area or avoid it.

Think about yourself.

What are your strengths?

What are your weaknesses?

> "Build up your weaknesses until they become your strong points."
>
> - Knute Rockne

How can you turn your weaknesses into your strong points?

"If human beings are perceived as potentials rather than problems, as possessing strengths instead of weaknesses, as unlimited rather that dull and unresponsive, then they thrive and grow to their capabilities."

- Barbara Bush

What does this quote tell you about why you should think positively about yourself? Write a short essay or a poem to share how this quote can apply to your own life.

Goals

"The world makes way for the man who knows where he is going."

- Ralph Waldo Emerson

Setting goals can help you overcome whatever life throws at you. Having goals gives you a sense of purpose and something to take your mind off the struggles you may face. To get anywhere, you have to know where you want to end up.

Take a look at the stories of these two students:

Sarai was in a life-threatening accident. A drunk driver ran a red light and plowed into the side of the car she was riding in. She spent a month in the hospital with burns, cuts and bruises all over her body and with two broken legs. When she got out of the hospital, she still couldn't put weight on her legs and was sore from the accident. Sarai was frustrated. She missed most of the basketball season. She couldn't go out with her friends. Whenever people came to visit, Sarai complained about how much pain she was in and how she hated her life. Eventually, her friends stopped visiting, and Sarai became depressed.

Around the same time, Jaleel was playing basketball with his friends. A player threw the ball out of bounds, and Jaleel went after it. Not thinking to look before he crossed the street, Jaleel darted in front of a speeding car. He, too, had broken bones, cuts and bruises. Jaleel could not wait to get out of the hospital. He told his mom he would be home in two weeks, and he was. Instead of sitting at home feeling sorry for himself, he set a goal to be back at school within a month and worked hard to make sure he would be caught up with his schoolwork when he got back. Even though his leg was broken in two places, Jaleel told his doctor he wanted to play basketball again within two months. His doctor was skeptical, but the physical therapist helped Jaleel work hard and, sure enough, he was back on the court in that two-month time frame.

1. What was the difference in the ways Sarai and Jaleel approached their setbacks?

2. How do you think setting goals helped Jaleel?

3. What are some goals Sarai could have set?

Effective Goal-Setting

In order for goal-setting to be successful, the goals you set should meet the following characteristics:

1. A combination of short-term and long-term goals
2. Specific
3. Realistic
4. Measurable
5. Relevant
6. Time-sensitive

Combining short-term goals with long-term goals helps keep you motivated. As you reach your short-term goals, you will be motivated to reach your long-term goals.

Goals must be specific. The less specific the goal, the less likely you are to reach it or to feel satisfied when you do. If you have a learning disability, do not set a goal to do better in school. Instead, set a goal to get a passing grade on your next math test or to make honor roll for the 3rd quarter.

Making your goals measurable and time-sensitive helps you to meet them. If you want to save money to help your mom pay the bills, set a goal to save $500 in three months. Goals without measurable results will not be effective. If goals are not time-sensitive, you can keep putting them off without consequence, making it harder to reach them.

Write six goals about anything. Include goals that meet the six characteristics above and those that do not. Then cross out the goals that do not meet those characteristics.

1.

2.

3.

4.

5.

6.

Setting Short-Term Goals

Short-term goals are designed to be completed quickly. You may set a goal to be completed in a few weeks or a few months. No short-term goal should last longer than six months.

What are some examples of short-term goals?

- o If you have just immigrated to the United States, your goal may be to find a conversation partner at school to help you learn English.
- o If you have recently lost a parent, your goal may be to find a support group within two months to help you positively work through your grief.
- o If you are homeless, your goal may be to find a place to live within a week or two.
- o If you have a disability, your goal may be to follow a more strenuous exercise routine or to learn a new skill within a month.

You may set short-term goals that connect with your long-term goals. These are often called enabling goals because meeting them enables you to meet your long-term goals as well.

What are some examples of enabling goals?

- o If you are gay, you may set an enabling goal to tell a friend before you tell your parents or come out publicly.
- o If you have dropped out of middle school, an enabling goal may be to enroll in a high school credit-recovery course or to read a certain number of pages in a GED prep book each day before going back to school or getting your GED.
- o If you have been arrested, an enabling goal may be to write a letter of apology to any victims of your crime as a step in turning your life around.
- o If you've found out that you're pregnant, an enabling goal may be to attend all of your classes, even when you start to show, to make sure you stay in school after you have the baby.

Take a moment and read about Quentin:

Quentin is in 8th grade. His long-term goal is to become an engineer, but he has a learning disability and does not have the grades right now to qualify for college scholarships. He lives with his mom, who is a single parent. She works a minimum-wage job and cannot afford to pay for college for Quentin.

What are some short-term or enabling goals Quentin can set to help him meet his long-term goal?

Setting Your Own Short-Term Goals

What are some things you would like to accomplish in the next few weeks or months? To help yourself come up with ideas, think about what you would like to accomplish personally, academically, emotionally, financially, at home, at school or with friends.

Take this opportunity to set a few short-term goals.

Short-Term Goal	How to Reach the Goal	Time Frame

Setting Long-Term Goals

A long-term goal is any goal that will take you six months or longer to complete. You may set long-term goals for a period as short as six months or for much longer periods of time. The length of the long-term goal does not matter as long as you have created a plan to help you reach that goal.

Take a moment to read about Jackson:

Jackson is in foster care. It's hard for him to set goals because while his foster parents are nice, he knows all too well that he may not be in the same place next week, next month or next year. He also knows that when he turns 18, he'll be on his own. That means he has two years to figure things out. His social worker suggested that he set some goals to help him prepare for that transition, so he came up with the following goals to reach by his 18th birthday:

1. Graduate high school
2. Go to college
3. Get a car

Now that he has his goals, he needs a plan to reach them. Let's look at the plans Jackson came up with to meet his goals.

Long-Term Goal: Graduate high school

Enabling Goal	Plan to Meet Goal	Time Frame
Make sure I'll have enough credits	Talk to school counselor	1 week
	Pass all my classes	Ongoing
Attend school	Get perfect attendance award next quarter and try for it every quarter.	1 quarter
	If not perfect attendance, allow only 5 missed days per quarter	Ongoing
Pass all my classes	Do my homework each night	Daily
	Get a planner to write assignments in	Ongoing
	Find a tutor to help me with classes I'm struggling in	Ongoing

Long-Term Goal: Go to College

Enabling Goal	Plan to Meet Goal	Time Frame
Find scholarships to pay for college	Talk with school counselor about scholarship opportunities now and in the future Research scholarships online Get grades up to qualify for scholarships	1 week Ongoing Ongoing
Fill out college applications	Start practicing filling out applications Visit schools to decide which ones to apply to	1 year 1 year
Take the ACT and SAT	Get study books from the library Take the ACT/SAT prep classes offered at school	1 year 1 year

Long-Term Goal: Get a Car

Enabling Goal	Plan to Meet Goal	Time Frame
Get a job	Fill out applications at 5 different places each week until I get a job Ask teachers and social worker to be references	1 month
Save at least $100 a month	Do not spend money on silly things Get a savings account	Ongoing 1 week
Find a good used car to buy	Figure out what type of car I want Browse used car ads to determine how much that car will cost	Weekly Weekly

You may have noticed that some of Jackson's goals do not have specific time frames. If your long-term goal has a set time frame, sometimes your enabling goals can be a little less specific. At the same time, if your enabling goals are specific, your long-term goal may not need as specific of a time frame.

For example, Jackson's long-term goal is to buy a car. His enabling goal says he wants to save $100 a month. He will not be able to specify when he can buy that car until he gets a job, determines how much the car will cost and finds someone selling an acceptable car.

What Are Your Long-Term Goals?

Come up with at least three long-term goals. Your goals may be similar to Jackson's, or you may want to go a different route. Instead of focusing on school, maybe you want to rebuild your parents' trust or develop healthy ways to express your anger. Maybe you want to make new friends or learn how to speak a new language. All of these things take time.

My long-term goals are…

1.

2.

3.

Now that you have written down those goals, you need to make a plan for reaching them. Fill in the chart just like Jackson did with a plan for meeting your goals.

Long-Term Goal: _____

Enabling Goal	Plan to Reach Goal	Time Frame

Long-Term Goal: _____

Enabling Goal	Plan to Reach Goal	Time Frame

Long-Term Goal: _____

Enabling Goal	Plan to Reach Goal	Time Frame

Reaching Your Goals

You've just taken a big step toward reaching your goals by writing them down. Studies have shown that people who write down their goals are more likely to reach those goals than people who do not. Other steps that help people reach their goals are:

- Set realistic, measurable goals (you already did that too!).
- Use a mix of short-term and long-term goals (you're 3 for 3!).
- Tell someone else about your goals.
- Visualize reaching your goals.

Do you have someone you can share your goals with? It could be a friend, a family member, a social worker, a counselor, a pastor. Look for someone who has your best interest in mind. It does not have to be someone you are extremely close with, just someone you know will help keep you on the right track.

I am going to share my goals with _____.

The final step toward reaching your goals is visualizing yourself reaching them. How do you do that? Here are a few ways:

- Take your goal and turn it into an "I am" phrase and repeat it to yourself every day. For example, "I am a high school graduate" or "I am a great English speaker."
- Go to a quiet place, close your eyes and think of yourself after you have reached your goals. If your goal is to graduate high school, you may visualize your graduation ceremony. If your goal is to learn English, you may visualize yourself having a conversation with a stranger.
- Draw a picture of yourself after you meet your goal.
- Make a large poster of your goals and put it where you will see it every morning.
- Write down all the good things that will come from meeting your goals.

Take a moment and use one of these strategies to visualize meeting your goal.

What strategy did you use?

How did it make you feel?

Other Ways to Be Resilient

By having something to look forward to, you have less time to let the hardships of life bring you down, but setting goals is just one of many ways to help you learn how to develop resilience. The more of these strategies and attitudes you develop, the easier it will be to become a resilient person.

Some of the ways to be resilient include:

- Developing rituals and routines
- Prioritizing tasks
- Juggling emotions and responsibilities
- Being optimistic
- Gaining control of a situation
- Learning to express yourself
- Handling stress properly
- Finding people to confide in
- Staying healthy
- Setting boundaries
- Using conflict-resolution strategies

Can you add anything to the list? What healthy strategies have you used to overcome challenges and difficult life situations in the past?

> "Adversity is a fact of life. It can't be controlled. What we can control is how we react to it."
>
> - Unknown

Celebrity Spotlight: Magic Johnson

In the 1980s and early '90s, Earvin "Magic" Johnson was a star in the NBA. In his rookie season, he not only won a championship but was also named the league's Most Valuable Player. From there he went on to help the Los Angeles Lakers win multiple championships. While he will be forever known as one of the greatest players in NBA history, Johnson will also be known for something else.

In 1991, Johnson announced that he had HIV and retired from basketball. While he came back to play in the 1992 Olympic Games and won a gold medal there, he started to move his focus from playing basketball to educating people about the risk of HIV/AIDS and the need to practice safe sex.

When Johnson contracted HIV/AIDS, very little was known about the disease. He faced players afraid to be on the court with him for fear they would also contract the disease. To help change those notions and promote HIV/AIDS research, Johnson started the Magic Johnson Foundation. Today, the foundation is his main focus. He will have to live with HIV the rest of his life, but he can handle it because he knows he's helping prevent the same outcome for others.

A few words of wisdom from Magic Johnson:

"All kids need is a little help, a little hope and somebody who believes in them."

"When you face a crisis, you know who your true friends are."

"I want to be here for a long time, so I am going to do everything I have to do to be here. And I want to walk my daughter down the aisle and give her away to somebody someday. I want to make sure I am still here to make sure my two young sons become men."

You can learn a lot from celebrities and others who have developed resilience and overcome adversity. Magic Johnson is unique because unlike a lot of situations, he has to live with his adversity on a daily basis. There is no cure for HIV/AIDS. If you have cancer or another life-threatening disease or know someone who does, you may feel the same way.

> "The first year was hard for me to deal with. The second year was a little bit easier, but still difficult. It took me five years to get it out of me. It was a difficult moment, a difficult time."
>
> -   Magic Johnson

What does this quote tell you about what it's like to live with adversity and the time it takes to develop resilience?

> "I tell you, it's funny because the only time I think about HIV is when I have to take my medicine twice a day."
>
> -   Magic Johnson

What does this quote mean? What does it tell you about how Magic Johnson handles his illness?

Developing Rituals and Routines

Rituals and routines are actions or sets of actions that we do on a regular basis. You may follow a certain routine when you get up in the morning. Your family may have certain rituals they follow during the holidays, such as always serving the same meal or setting up the Christmas tree on a specific day.

What are some of your rituals and routines?

How can having rituals and routines help you develop resilience and overcome adversity? By giving you some stability. No matter what problems you are facing, chances are there's a lack of stability. If you're homeless, you may not know where you'll sleep tonight. If you've recently lost a parent, life is a lot different than it used to be. If you're dependent on drugs, the effect of those substances will make your life even more unstable.

When you follow rituals and routines, you bring elements into your life that you can depend on when times get rough. If those rituals and routines are interrupted, you can create new ones to help you cope with the adversity you face. When life is full of change, you need something you can count on.

If you do not have rituals and routines, think of the things in your life that remain the same. These constants can help you get through the tumultuous times.

Take one of your rituals, routines or constants and write a short poem about it.

Prioritizing Tasks

Part of developing rituals and routines and setting goals is determining what tasks and what people are most important on a daily basis. What's most important to you? Doing well in school? Spending time with friends? Learning to play an instrument? Participating in a club, a band or a special hobby? Exercising and staying healthy?

List the ten things you do every week that are most important to you or mean the most to you.

1.

2.

3.

4.

5.

6.

7.

8.

9.

10.

Now list the ten things you spend the most time on every week.

1.

2.

3.

4.

5.

6.

7.

8.

9.

10.

Do your two lists match up? You may have a few things on the second list that you cannot really change, such as eating, getting dressed or going to school. But do you also have activities on the second list that you wish weren't there or that you wish you spent less time on?

Look at Yolanda's two lists:

The Ten Things I Do Every Week that Are Most Important to Me

1. Eating dinner with my family
2. Playing volleyball
3. Student council sessions
4. Shopping with my mom
5. Hanging out with my friends
6. Watching my favorite show on TV
7. Playing games with my sister
8. Doing my homework
9. Talking to my parents
10. Going running

The Ten Things I Spend the Most Time On

1. Getting ready for school
2. Arguing with my sister
3. Sleeping
4. Moping in my room
5. Watching TV
6. Going running
7. Listening to music
8. Using Facebook
9. Texting friends
10. Playing volleyball

1. Do the things that are most important to Yolanda match up with the things she spends the most time on?

2. What are some changes Yolanda could make to her priorities?

Like Yolanda, Jared found that his list of what was most important didn't match up with the things he spent the most time on. Take a look at Jared's lists:

The Things that Are Most Important to Me

1. Spending time with my family
2. Spending time with my friends
3. Going to school
4. Playing baseball
5. Going to church
6. Exercising and staying healthy
7. Looking my best
8. Relaxing and watching TV
9. Spending time online
10. Writing

The Things I Spend the Most Time On

1. Hanging out in my room
2. Avoiding my parents
3. Trying to talk to my friends
4. Staying home from school and playing video games
5. Sitting on the bench at baseball games
6. Sleeping
7. Writing in my journal
8. Reading Facebook messages and comments
9. Looking my best
10. Pretending to be sick

You may notice that Jared does not do most of the things that are important to him. Many of the things he does spend time on are negative. Jared recently came out to his parents and his friends. They were all less supportive than he had hoped they would be. The other players on the baseball team make fun of him and leave the locker room whenever he walks in. He is harassed at school and pretends to be sick so he can stay home. When he goes online, he spends most of his time looking at his friends' Facebook pages, missing them and reading comments that bullies leave on his page. He's starting to hate his life and hate himself, but he doesn't know what to do.

What can Jared do to overcome his situation?

Take another look at your own list.

1. If there are things that are important to you that you do not spend a lot of time on, what can you change to make more time for those things?

2. Are there any negative behaviors or activities on your second list? If so, what causes them? What can you do to get rid of them?

When you refocus your priorities and spend time on what's important to you, it is easier to be resilient. This may mean cutting back the time you spend with friends who are bad influences to spend more time with your family. If you receive negative messages online, you may want to cut back your computer use and focus on talking to people who make you feel good about yourself. If you spend time doing drugs or feeling depressed, ask someone you trust for help. Doing something for someone else or taking up a new hobby may help you feel better too.

Juggling Emotions and Responsibilities

Sometimes your negative emotions can keep you from dealing with your responsibilities. Other times, they can spur you to action. As you learn to be resilient and overcome adversity, you have to learn to handle your negative emotions positively so they do not keep you from fulfilling your responsibilities.

The two stories below show both ends of the spectrum:

Kam's Story

Kam's dad is abusive. He verbally abuses Kam and his younger siblings, telling them that they're not wanted and that they will never amount to anything. He hits Kam's mother whenever she doesn't do something up to his standards, which seems to happen on a daily basis. Kam wants to beat up his dad for hitting his mom and to yell back at him whenever he verbally abuses Kam and his siblings. Even though Kam is angry at his dad, he does not fight back because he knows it would only make things worse.

Kam feels responsible for taking care of his siblings and his mom. He channels his anger into working hard at school and making as much money as possible with his after-school job. His goal is for his mom to leave his dad, but he knows with no money and no help, she will not agree to it. He's working with a school counselor to help change her mind. The thought of being able to help out his mom and his siblings makes it easier for him to take his dad's abuse.

Alicia's Story

When her mom died, Alicia sank into a depression. Her friend suggested she try marijuana to ease the pain. She liked how it made her relax and forget her troubles, so she got into a regular habit of smoking with her friends after school and on the weekends. She didn't think about how doing drugs would affect her dad and sister at home until her sister met her at the door one day. "I miss you, Alicia," she said. Alicia knew that she needed to be there for her sister and be a good role model, but the depression was too much to handle, so she kept up her drug use and grew more and more distant from her dad and sister.

1. What could Alicia have done instead of turning to drugs?

2. How did Kam turn his negative emotions into a positive?

3. How have you handled your emotions when you've had a difficult situation with your family?

Celebrity Spotlight: J.K. Rowling

You probably know J.K. Rowling as the author of the *Harry Potter* series, but it's likely you do not know the struggles she went through before finding success.

Before publishing the *Harry Potter* series, Rowling was a single mother contemplating suicide. Without a job and with a failed marriage, Rowling felt like she would never make anything of herself. Instead of letting depression and financial troubles take over her life, Rowling poured her emotions and energy into finishing *Harry Potter*. Once the book was finished, she submitted it to 12 publishers and all of them rejected it. Thirteen proved to be Rowling's lucky number. On the 13th try, her book was finally accepted by a publisher and became the thing that would turn her into a billionaire.

In June 2008, Rowling was asked to give the commencement address at Harvard University. Her speech to the graduates included the following bits of wisdom to help you as you work toward developing resilience:

"Ultimately, we all have to decide for ourselves what constitutes failure, but the world is quite eager to give you a set of criteria if you let it."

"Failure gave me an inner security that I had never attained by passing examinations. Failure taught me things about myself that I could have learned no other way. I discovered that I had a strong will, and more discipline than I had suspected; I also found out that I had friends whose value was truly above the price of rubies."

"Life is difficult, and complicated, and beyond anyone's total control, and the humility to know that will enable you to survive its vicissitudes."

"We do not need magic to change the world. We carry all the power we need inside ourselves already: we have the power to imagine better."

The Power of Optimism

Studies have been done to show the power of optimism in overcoming adversity and recovering from illness. Multiple studies have shown that optimistic thinking has been a key factor in cancer survival rates. Even patients with terminal cancer who were optimistic lived significantly longer than those who just gave up.

Being optimistic doesn't mean you're never going to have negative thoughts, feel upset or get depressed. It means that you don't let the negatives consume you. That's hard work sometimes, especially when it seems like you're being hit with one negative after another or are stuck in a situation that feels like it will never end.

Try some of these strategies to overcome negativity and develop an attitude of optimism:

1. Choose to wake up on the right side of the bed every morning.
2. Rid your life of people and activities that bring negativity into your life.
3. Take care of yourself by eating well, getting enough sleep and exercising.
4. Keep a collection of motivational quotes or sayings.
5. Take time to participate in positive activities you enjoy.
6. Do something nice for someone else.
7. Seek out humor: watch a funny movie, read some jokes, act silly.
8. Listen to upbeat music.
9. Be flexible.
10. Focus on your successes and learn from your failures.

Which of these strategies do you think could help you most?

Why is being optimistic such a powerful force?

Melania's Story

Melania couldn't believe it. She'd been out with some friends when a couple of them decided to shoplift from one of the hottest new stores in the mall. She told her friends not to do it, but they didn't listen. When the alarm rang, her best friend, Ericka, shoved one of the stolen items into Melania's hands. Next thing she knew, security guards were escorting her away. Even though she hadn't been in trouble before, no one believed that she was innocent. The security cameras couldn't tell who had actually picked up the items, so Melania was found guilty. The judge sentenced her to three months in a juvenile detention center to teach her a lesson.

The juvenile detention center wasn't as bad as she had anticipated it would be, but it still wasn't fun. For the first month, Melania was down on herself and couldn't believe what had happened to her. She kept to herself, ignored phone calls and letters from family and friends and started to sink into a deep depression. During a counseling session, her social worker decided to set her straight.

"Look, Melania. I know you say you didn't do it. Whether you did or didn't shoplift isn't the point here. The fact is you're here now, and you'll be here for the next two months. What are you going to do to make the most of that time?"

Melania thought about what her social worker said and realized she was right. There was nothing she could do to change her circumstances at the moment, but she could make the best out of a bad situation. From that day on, her attitude changed. She woke up each day with a positive attitude. She participated in the exercise opportunities and activities that were offered for the girls at the center. Instead of sitting in the corner during group counseling, she participated with the other girls.

When it came time for her to leave the detention center, Melania knew she had to make some changes in her life. She wrote a letter to Ericka and told her why they could not be friends anymore. She sent her parents and Ericka's parents copies of a letter Ericka had written asking Melania to forgive her for what she did and put the rest behind her.

Melania walked out of the juvenile detention center a changed person. She knew she shouldn't have been sent there in the first place, but she didn't stay bitter about it. Instead, she focused on the positive lessons she learned while there and focused on the newfound strength she had developed.

How did the power of optimism help Melania handle a bad situation?

Celebrity Spotlight: J.R. Martinez

A lot of people had never heard of J.R. Martinez until he competed on, and won, *Dancing With the Stars* in 2011, but Martinez's biggest struggle did not come from trying to win a dancing competition. In 2003, while deployed with the Army to the Middle East, the Humvee he was driving was hit by a roadside bomb. The bomb left Martinez with burns on over 40% of his body. It took him nearly three years and 33 surgeries to recover.

Martinez did not let his condition bring him down. Doctors and nurses recognized his resilience and asked him to speak to other burn patients. He turned those short, one-on-one talks into larger motivational speaking engagements. He also joined the Phoenix Society for Burn Survivors to bring more support to those with traumatic injuries and disfiguration from burns.

While Martinez's face will never look the same, his spirit will continue to persevere.

A few words of wisdom from J.R. Martinez:

"Despite what you may go through in life, you never quit. You have hope and you have patience and you dream, because if you can do those things, you can accomplish anything in life."

"Scars go beyond what the physical eye can catch and deep into the veins as it runs simultaneously with your blood. It filters through the body and even into the brain, as it affects how our men and women integrate back into a quote-unquote 'normal life'."

"I believe my physical scars are my new uniform and my words are my new weapon."

Expressing Yourself

Being optimistic and developing resilience isn't about holding your emotions in. In fact, when you hide your emotions and refuse to tell people how you really feel, it can be harder to be positive and endure difficult situations. Learning to express your emotions in healthy ways can make situations easier to handle and can help you gain control over those emotions.

Negative Ways to Handle Your Emotions

Do you handle your emotions in any of the following negative ways?

- Becoming withdrawn and depressed
- Turning to drugs and alcohol
- Getting angry and yelling/screaming
- Becoming violent
- Throwing things
- Throwing up
- Self-harm

If you have handled your emotions negatively, how did that make you feel?

Instead of the negative actions above, try expressing your emotions in the following positive ways:

- Talking it out with someone
- Writing a letter
- Channeling your emotions into a positive activity
- Meditating or using another relaxation strategy
- Keeping your cool
- Finding something to laugh about

Put yourself in the shoes of these teens. Read each scenario and explain how you would positively handle the emotions you'd feel in these situations.

1. Zoe was recently expelled from school for getting into a fight with another girl. She's mad at the girl for picking the fight and mad at the principal for not giving her another chance. She's depressed because she thinks she'll never finish school.

2. Jorge was recently diagnosed with cancer. His friends are afraid to be around him and his doctor told him he can't play soccer anymore. He's bored, lonely and scared.

3. Cat's mom just kicked her dad out of the house for having an affair. Cat's mad at her dad for ruining their family, mad at her mom for not doing more to keep her dad from having an affair and sad that her family is falling apart.

4. Ram just moved to the United States. In school, kids tease him because of his accent and ask if he's a terrorist because of how he looks. He's becoming embarrassed of his family and his heritage.

5. Max has been in and out of foster homes his entire life. He just wants someone to love him and pay attention to him, so he acts out by stealing and vandalizing public property.

Creating a Support Network

In order to talk out your emotions and feel secure, you need to build a support network. Your support network should be made up of positive influences and people you can go to when you're feeling sad, depressed, overwhelmed or angry. The people in your support network should all have your best interest in mind.

Who can be in your support network?

- Friends
- Parents
- Other family members
- Teachers
- Counselors
- Pastors
- Church members

You need to trust the members of your support network enough to share what you're feeling. They cannot help you if you're not honest with them.

Right now, think of at least ten people who could be a part of your support network. If you have trouble thinking of ten people you know well, it's okay to include people who do not know you very well but are still a positive influence in your life, such as teachers or the school counselor.

1.

2.

3.

4.

5.

6.

7.

8.

9.

10.

If you can think of more than ten, that's okay too. The more people in your network, the more people you will have to go to when you face problems.

The Constant that I Need

"I'll always be there for you," she said.
And it's true, she always was.
Always the first to wipe my tears
And the first with her applause.
I never really understood
Why she was always there.
When other things mattered more
She's the one who always cared.

Of course it wasn't always good.
I didn't like her on my case.
I told her just to back away
And get out of my face.
I didn't need her there for me.
I could do it on my own.
She went away and I soon found
That I was all alone.

Only when I was all alone
Did I realize what I'd lost.
It wasn't like I thought it'd be
I didn't like the cost.
And so I went crawling back to her
Tears streaming from my eyes.
I told her I was sorry
And she just looked at me and sighed.

"I'll always be there for you," she said.
And it's true, she always was.
Always the first to wipe my tears
And the first with her applause.
Even when I forget
Just how much she means
She's always waiting for my return.
The constant that I need.

1. What lesson did the speaker of this poem learn?

2. Why was the person the speaker mentions in the poem important?

3. Do you have anyone in your life who resembles the person the speaker references in the poem?

Resources for Finding Support

Look to these groups to help you find support for whatever you may be going through.

Addiction
Alcoholics Anonymous
AddictionSurvivors.org
SMART Recovery
Free Addiction Helpline (877) 259-5634
National Council on Alcoholism and Drug
   Dependency (800) NCA-CALL
 	
Suicide
National Suicide Prevention Lifeline
(800) 273-TALK
Youth Suicide Prevention Program
SAVE.org
Local mental-health agencies and suicide
   hotlines
800-SUICIDE
 	
Grief
Local churches
Local hospitals
Hospice
Griefshare.org
 	
Eating Disorders
National Eating Disorders Association
Local hospitals and mental-health agencies
National Mental Health America
	Rape and Abuse
	RAINN – Rape, Abuse, Incest National
	   Network
	National Sexual Assault Hotline
	   (800) 656-HOPE
	National Domestic Violence Helpline
	   (866)331-9474
	ChildHelp USA
	   (800) 422-4453
	
	Illness
	Hospice
	Local hospital programs
	Grief support programs
	
	GLBT Issues
	LYRIC (800) 246-PRIDE
	PFLAG
	Anti-Hate Line (800) 649-0404
	
	Other Issues
	National Runaway Hotline
	   (800) 621-4000
	America's Pregnancy Hotline
	   (888) 672-2296
	SAFE (Self-Abuse Finally Ends)
	   (800) DONT-CUT
	Disabilities/Handicapped Crisis Line
	   (800) 626-HAND

Setting Boundaries

> "Boundaries are to protect life – not limit pleasures."
>
> - Edwin Louis Cole

Setting boundaries for yourself can help you develop resilience and keep you from encountering situations that trigger negative attitudes, emotions or behaviors. Your boundaries may include avoiding certain people or places, talking with someone in your support network before making key decisions or making sure you are always around others so that you're not tempted to engage in negative behaviors.

Determine the boundaries that you need to set by answering these questions:

1. What activities have a negative effect, cause negative emotions or turn you into someone you don't like?

2. What people have a negative influence on you?

3. What places bring out the worst in you or tempt you to behave in negative ways?

4. What times of the day, the week, the month or the year are the toughest for you?

5. What triggers negative emotions in you?

Use these answers to determine your boundaries. When writing your boundaries, begin with phrases such as "I will…," "I will not…" or "Others will not…" Examples of boundaries include "I will not associate with people who smoke or drink" or "Others will not raise their voices with me."

Come up with three boundaries to start with.

1.

2.

3.

Sticking to your boundaries is hard work. You have to learn how to tell people "no," tell people when they have crossed a line and walk away from situations that come close to crossing the boundaries you have set for yourself. If your boundaries include cutting out people who have a negative influence on you, you can expect that people will ridicule you and try to make you feel guilty about your decision.

Share your boundaries with the members of your support network. They will be the people who back you up and praise you for sticking to your boundaries. They will also remind you of your boundaries when you're in danger of crossing them.

Do not be discouraged if you find yourself crossing your boundaries at first. When you're not used to having boundaries, it can be difficult to follow them. Gradually, you will learn to stick to your boundaries. As you do, you may discover other people, places and situations that trigger negative emotions and behaviors. Add to your boundaries and revise them as necessary. As you develop resilience, you may find that you no longer need your initial boundaries.

Celebrity Spotlight: Steven Tyler

Steven Tyler, the lead singer for Aerosmith and a former *American Idol* judge, is no stranger to addiction and adversity. While he is now sober, he has openly admitted his battles with drugs and alcohol and the effects those addictions have had on his life. Because of his addictions, Tyler contracted Hepatitis C, a disease that can be caused by drug use through intravenous needles. His drug use also caused the end of at least one of his marriages.

The consequences Tyler has faced have helped him develop resilience and work harder to overcome his addiction. How does he stay away from drugs and keep his addictions from getting the best of him? He sets boundaries. In 2009, Tyler became addicted to pain-killers after undergoing a medical procedure. That addiction, coupled with everything he had lost, made him realize that he had to set boundaries and be aware of himself in order to avoid more addictions.

Today, Tyler will tout his sobriety but admits that it takes work. He has a support network that includes two Alcoholics Anonymous sponsors. While he may not be able to avoid pain-killers and prescribed medications, he can use his support network to keep him sober and help him stay in control.

A few words of wisdom from Steven Tyler:

"Drugs will get you out of your own way, but we lived it, and that's dangerous. It can actually turn around on itself and steal your soul, and that's what happened."

"Every life has a measure of sorrow, and sometimes this is what awakens us."

Conflict Resolution

Learning healthy ways to resolve conflict can help you stick to your boundaries and become more resilient.

What do you do when something makes you angry or when someone does something you don't like?

Responses to conflict typically fall in one of three areas:

- Passive
- Aggressive
- Assertive

Passive Response to Conflict

When you respond to conflict passively, you don't deal with it. Instead, you ignore the conflict, hide how you may be feeling or react nonverbally.

Aggressive Response to Conflict

When you respond to conflict aggressively, you deal with the conflict negatively and may not resolve anything. You yell. You call people names. You hit. You throw things or slam doors. You make threats.

Assertive Response to Conflict

When you respond to conflict assertively, you work to resolve the conflict. You listen to all sides of the story and apologize if you were at fault. You express how the conflict made you feel and act politely while talking it out.

Read the following scenarios and determine how the teen handled the conflict. If the teen handled the conflict passively or aggressively, suggest assertive ways the conflict could have been handled.

When Marisol's classmates found out she was a lesbian, the harassment started almost instantly. Whenever her classmates called Marisol a name or made an offensive comment, she didn't let them get away with it. She would call them another offensive name right back, but it didn't stop the harassment. Classmates started picking on Marisol more just to hear her response.

Jill's best friend, Rebekah, committed suicide. A lot of rumors started to spread about why Rebekah committed suicide, and even their other friends started talking negatively about Rebekah. The comments and rumors made Jill extremely mad. Whenever she heard something bad about Rebekah, she started spreading rumors about others and sent her classmates anonymous letters to try and make them feel bad.

Syrian was caught stealing from a major department store. The judge sent him to a juvenile detention center for a few months. When he got back to school, other kids would make comments like, "Hide your valuables! Syrian's here!" Whenever something came up missing in school, Syrian was the first one accused. Instead of trying to prove his innocence or explaining that he had changed, Syrian acted out in anger. He yelled at kids. He threatened to fight them. He got in a lot more trouble.

Conflict-Resolution Strategies

If you find yourself using passive or aggressive strategies for dealing with conflict in your life, try some of these strategies to deal with conflict more positively.

Resolving Conflict with Others

1. Bring in a third party to help you deal with the conflict. Use a counselor, a teacher or a peer mediator. You want someone who will listen to the facts before giving an opinion.

2. Use "I" statements to acknowledge your feelings. Say something along the lines of, "When X happened, I felt…"

3. Take time to chill out before dealing with the conflict.

4. Focus on the problem, not what's wrong with you or anyone else involved.

Resolving Conflict with Yourself

1. Forget the past and focus on living in the present and moving forward.

2. Don't worry about what other people think.

3. Listen to your intuition.

4. Use "I" statements with yourself to identify how certain conflicts make you feel.

5. Think about how you can make your life and your world better.

Think about a current conflict in your life that you have put off dealing with or a past conflict that you handled poorly. How could you use these strategies to deal with that conflict?

Celebrity Spotlight: Demi Lovato

Demi Lovato had a lot going for her. She had a hit Disney Channel show, *Sonny with a Chance*, and a budding music career. She starred in Disney's *Camp Rock* movies and was dating a Jonas Brother. What more could a teenager ask for? But even celebrities don't have it easy, and Lovato was no exception.

Despite her fame, Lovato has had to face her inner demons. She famously went to rehab after breaking up with Joe Jonas and getting in a fight with a backup dancer. Since then, Lovato has admitted to having an eating disorder and an addiction to cutting herself. Lovato also admitted to self-medicating and using alcohol and drugs to ease her pain.

While Lovato works to rise up from her addictions, she will be the first to admit that the battle is long and difficult. By openly talking about her struggles and becoming an advocate for other teens who face eating disorders and other problems, Lovato is gaining strength and demonstrating resilience as she fights her inner demons.

A few words of wisdom from Demi Lovato:

"Sometimes being afraid can show more strength than being fearless."

"When you've got good friends and family around you, you don't feel the need to go off the deep end."

"The way I want to be a role model is not by not making mistakes, but by helping people overcome things from the obstacles that I've overcome."

"There's no point to living life unless you make history, and the best way to make history is to help others."

Developing Character Traits

When you're faced with a crisis, adversity and other situations that require resilience, certain character traits can help you face that adversity and develop resilience.

Caring

> "Caring about others, running the risk of feeling, and leaving an impact on people, brings happiness."
>
> -   Harold Kushner

Do you agree with the quote from Harold Kushner?

When you step outside of yourself and your problems to show care for others, you take the focus off your problems and refocus your energy into helping others. No matter how big your problem, someone always has a problem that is bigger.

This is not meant to minimize your struggles. Often when you face adversity or are in crisis, your life loses a sense of purpose. Caring helps bring that sense of purpose back.

Look for ways to demonstrate caring that relate to your problems. Has a parent died? Join a support group with other teens who have lost parents and care about each other. Are you working to overcome an addiction? Dedicate time to helping other teens overcome addictions as well.

Think about your life and your current situation. What are some ways you can care for others?

A Story of Caring

Alex's Lemonade Stand is a charity that raises money for cancer research, but it wasn't started by just anyone. At age one, Alex Scott was diagnosed with a rare form of cancer. By the time she was four years old, she knew she wanted to give something back to the doctors who had helped treat her cancer and perform her surgeries. Alex asked her parents if she could sell lemonade to raise money to help other kids with cancer. That lemonade stand raised $2,000.

Alex and her family continued to hold the lemonade stand each year until Alex passed away. In the four years that they held the lemonade stand, Alex and her family raised over $1 million for cancer research. The little girl turned her fight with cancer into an opportunity to care about others, but the story doesn't stop there.

When Alex passed away, her parents needed a way to work through their grief. They started the Alex's Lemonade Stand Foundation. Since 2004, their foundation has raised over $50 million for cancer research. It has attracted the attention of celebrities such as singer Jordin Sparks and model Cindy Crawford. Lemonade stands have been set up throughout the United States to raise money for cancer research, and Alex's legacy lives on.

1. How do you think Alex's Lemonade Stand helped Alex and her parents through Alex's battle with cancer?

2. What do you personally think about what they did?

3. How does this story demonstrate the power of caring?

Celebrity Spotlight: Tyler Perry

Tyler Perry, an African-American actor, director and playwright, is best known for his Madea movies, stage plays and productions that feature African-American actors. While he has experienced fame as an actor and director, it took a lot for him to get there.

During his childhood, Perry had a troubled relationship with his father. He faced regular abuse that eventually destroyed their relationship. Perry has also admitted to being sexually abused by family members as a child.

What does Perry credit with getting him through his tough times? Faith. Perry integrates his faith in God and strong character traits in many of his plays and movies. While sticking to strong morals and speaking up about believing in God isn't always popular, Perry doesn't care. He will not put aside what pulled him through adversity and helped him become the success he is today.

A few words of wisdom from Tyler Perry:

"People always try to do the right thing..after they've tried everything else."

"I didn't have a catharsis for my childhood pain. Most of us don't, and until I learned how to forgive those people and let it go, I was unhappy."

"Are you living or just existing?"

"Don't wait for someone to green-light your project. Build your own intersection."

"I know that there are a lot of people out there with stories far worse than mine, but you, too, can make it. To those of you who have, welcome to life. I celebrate you."

"I was a very poor young black boy in New Orleans, just a face without a name, swimming in a sea of poverty, trying to survive."

Equality

Take a look at these quotes about equality.

> "Don't be in a hurry to condemn because he doesn't do what you do or think as you think or as fast. There was a time when you didn't know what you know today."
>
> - Malcolm X

Does this quote remind you of any conflict or situations you have faced?

> The tears of the red, yellow, black, brown and white man are all the same.
>
> ~Martin H. Fischer

How can this quote help you as you're facing adversity or feeling like no one has ever gone through what you are going through?

> "I hate to complain...No one is without difficulties, whether in high or low life, and every person knows best where their own shoe pinches."
>
> - Abigail Adams

What does this quote from Abigail Adams say to you?

Often when you find yourself in a situation requiring resilience, you also find people who make you feel like an outcast, who are afraid to be around you or who ridicule you for the situation you're going through. Focusing on equality can help you develop resilience in two ways:

It reminds you that you are not alone in your struggles

To use equality as a reminder that you are not alone in your struggles, seek out other people who are facing similar challenges. If a support group does not exist for people who are going through similar struggles, create one. The goal of a support group is not to throw a large pity party for each other. It is to realize that you can use a spirit of equality and band together to build each other up and help each other get through your struggles together.

The Internet is a good place to look for others who are facing similar struggles. You do not have to meet with people face to face to support one another. Look for online support groups you can join. Do a search to find resources in your community or look for summer camps and retreats for people like you.

It gives you an opportunity to educate others

Maybe you have cancer or have been partially paralyzed and your friends are afraid to spend time with you. Maybe you are gay and feel isolated from your peers. By remembering that we are all equal and finding similarities between yourself and others, you can educate your peers.

This may involve reminding your friends that you're still the same person you were before being diagnosed with an illness or before being in an accident. It may involve starting a gay-straight alliance or another awareness group at your school to help students understand you better.

How can you use the idea of equality to help you through your struggles?

A Story About Equality

Ricky felt like he didn't belong. Since realizing he was gay, he had begun to feel like he was the only gay person in the world. Friends were afraid to be around him. Family members were upset with him. So many people wanted to fix him, but no one wanted to understand him. While looking for support online, Ricky found a summer camp for LGBT teens and decided maybe it would help.

At camp, Ricky no longer felt like he was the only gay person in the world. He was surrounded by teenagers who felt as isolated and alone as he did. They leaned on one another and learned how to support each other. Counselors taught them strategies for handling their negative feelings when they left camp and returned to their daily lives.

When he got home from camp, Ricky felt renewed. His friends and family members were still the same, but he handled it better. He had the names, phone numbers and email addresses of people who were going through the same things he was. Even though they didn't live in the same cities or even the same states, Ricky and his new friends supported each other and were helped by the realization that they were equals in a cause. They called each other regularly and emailed one another.

Through the support of his new friends, Ricky began to develop resilience. He was not as affected by the opinions of friends and the inability of those around him to understand what he was going through.

1. How did the realization that he was not alone help Ricky?

2. How do Ricky and his new friends help one another?

3. What else could Ricky do to feel like he's not alone?

Asset-Building

One trait that can help you develop resilience when you face financial struggles, such as living in poverty, being homeless or losing a parent and the financial support that parents provide, is learning how to be financially responsible. It can be hard to think about managing money when you don't have any, but there are ways to wisely use the money that you do have and ways to earn more money.

1. Set goals
   Use the goal-setting strategies discussed earlier in the workbook to come up with financial goals for yourself. Maybe your goal is to save a certain amount of money. Maybe you want to get a job. Maybe you want to buy something that will make life easier for your family. Whatever it is, keep your goals realistic. If you have $0, trying to earn $1,000 may be daunting, but $100 may not be quite as hard.

2. Do whatever you can (within reason) to earn money
   Do not focus on earning money with a traditional job. While getting a job at a fast-food place or a grocery store is a good idea if you're old enough, look for other ways to add to that. Offer to mow grass or run errands for a neighbor. Start a small house-cleaning service. Buy something at a discount and sell it to make a profit. A lot of teens have overcome adversity and improved their financial state by being creative when it comes to making money.

3. Save whatever you can
   Every little bit helps. When you get a little extra money, don't blow it on fast food, new clothes or something you don't really need. Save that little bit of extra money. A few dollars may not seem like much, but if you save a few dollars every month, you'll have a few hundred at the end of the year. That little bit of money will give you some peace of mind and security when problems arise.

Desiderata by Max Ehrmann

Go placidly amid the noise and the haste,
and remember what peace there may be in silence.

As far as possible, without surrender,
be on good terms with all persons.
Speak your truth quietly and clearly;
and listen to others,
even to the dull and the ignorant;
they too have their story.
Avoid loud and aggressive persons;
they are vexatious to the spirit.

If you compare yourself with others,
you may become vain or bitter,
for always there will be greater and lesser persons than yourself.
Enjoy your achievements as well as your plans.
Keep interested in your own career, however humble;
it is a real possession in the changing fortunes of time.

Exercise caution in your business affairs,
for the world is full of trickery.
But let this not blind you to what virtue there is;
many persons strive for high ideals,
and everywhere life is full of heroism.
Be yourself. Especially do not feign affection.
Neither be cynical about love,
for in the face of all aridity and disenchantment,
it is as perennial as the grass.

Take kindly the counsel of the years,
gracefully surrendering the things of youth.
Nurture strength of spirit to shield you in sudden misfortune.
But do not distress yourself with dark imaginings.
Many fears are born of fatigue and loneliness.

Beyond a wholesome discipline,
be gentle with yourself.
You are a child of the universe
no less than the trees and the stars;
you have a right to be here.
And whether or not it is clear to you,
no doubt the universe is unfolding as it should.

Therefore be at peace with God,
whatever you conceive Him to be.
And whatever your labors and aspirations,
in the noisy confusion of life,
keep peace with your soul.

With all its sham, drudgery, and broken dreams,
it is still a beautiful world.
Be cheerful. Strive to be happy.

1. The poem "Desiderata" is a highly popular motivational poem. How can this poem
    motivate you as you seek to develop resilience and overcome adversity?

2. What character traits does the poem promote?

3. "Nurture strength of spirit to shield you in sudden misfortune.
    But do not distress yourself with dark imaginings.
    Many fears are born of fatigue and loneliness."

    What do these lines mean, and how do they relate to being resilient?

Celebrity Spotlight: Oprah Winfrey

Oprah Winfrey is best known for motivating and inspiring women throughout the world. For 25 years, Winfrey helped others share their struggles and triumphs on *The Oprah Winfrey Show*. She also used the show to share her own struggles in life and describe how she worked to overcome them.

Winfrey's early life was anything but easy. She was born to a single mother and had to live with knowing she wasn't a planned child. She lived in a home where physical abuse occurred on a daily basis, and she was sexually abused as well. When she was 14, she became pregnant as the result of sexual abuse and gave birth to a stillborn baby.

While life wasn't easy and she encountered many negative influences, Winfrey credits the people who had a positive influence on her life for helping her overcome adversity and develop resilience. Who were those positive people? Her grandmother gave her strength. Her father set high standards. Her teachers instilled in her a love for learning and provided care and support.

Even after becoming famous, Winfrey's life was not free from struggles. She had to deal with family members trying to take advantage of her fame and had to convince herself that she was smart enough and talented enough to deserve the success she had received.

In addition to pouring her energy into her career, Winfrey has developed resilience through helping others. She became well-known for giving away elaborate gifts to members of her audience, including the famous "you're getting a new car" episode when she gave away a new car to every member of her audience. Winfrey also started Oprah's Angel Network, which has given millions of dollars to charities and nonprofit organizations throughout the world. In 2007, she opened a school in South Africa to help improve the lives of girls there.

Winfrey has gained a reputation as someone who has overcome a lot, has gained much wisdom from the process and has gone on to inspire millions of people throughout the world.

Words of Wisdom from Oprah Winfrey

"Turn your wounds into wisdom."

"For every one of us that succeeds, it's because there is somebody there to show you the way out. The light doesn't necessarily have to be in your family; for me it was teachers and school."

"I trust that everything happens for a reason, even if we are not wise enough to see it."

"Be thankful for what you have; you'll end up having more. If you concentrate on what you don't have, you will never, ever have enough. "

"Breathe. Let go. And remind yourself that this very moment is the only one you know you have for sure."

"My philosophy is that not only are you responsible for your life, but doing the best at this moment puts you in the best place for the next moment."

"I define joy as a sustained sense of well-being and internal peace - a connection to what matters."

"I know for sure that what we dwell on is who we become."

"Where there is no struggle, there is no strength."

"I am a woman in process. I'm just trying like everybody else. I try to take every conflict, every experience, and learn from it. Life is never dull."

"You are worthy because you are born. You are here. And you alone are enough."

Summing It Up

1. What is resilience?

2. How can you develop resilience?

3. What situations in your own life could benefit from your increased resilience?

4. "A revolution is a struggle between the future and the past" – Fidel Castro
    How does this quote connect to resilience?

5. Now what? Now that you've learned about resilience, what are you going to do? How is your life going to change?

Resources to Learn About Resilience

Reading stories about resilient teens, even if they are fictional, can help you develop resilience in yourself. Check out some of these books to help you.

Books About Addiction

Crank by Ellen Hopkins

Cut by Patricia McCormick

Books About Eating Disorders and Being Overweight

Wintergirls by Laurie Halse Anderson

Perfect by Natasha Friend

Second Star to the Right by Deborah Hautzig

I Am an Artichoke by Lucy Frank

I Was a 15-Year-Old Blimp by Patti Stren

Slob by Ellen Potter

Books About Suicide

The Burn Journals by Brent Runyon

It's Kind of a Funny Story by Ned Vizzini

Thirteen Reasons Why by Jay Asher

Impulse by Ellen Hopkins

Books About GLBT Issues

The Misfits by James Howe

Quimbaya by Dianne C. Stewart

Empress of the World by Sara Ryan

M or F? by Lisa Papademetriou and Chris Tebbetts

Books About Rape and Abuse

A Child Called "It": One Child's Courage to Survive by Dave Pelzer

Homecoming by Cynthia Voigt

Okay for Now by Gary Schmidt

Books About Illness and Grief

Angels in Pink series and other books by Lurlene McDaniel

One of Those Hideous Books Where the Mother Dies by Sonya Sones

Behind You by Jacqueline Woodson

Kiss the Morning Star by Elissa Janine Hoole

After Ever After by Jordan Sonnenblick

Books About Immigration and Different Cultures

Journey of the Sparrows by Fran Leeper Buss

Seedfolks by Paul Fleischman

A Step from Heaven by An Na

When I Was Puerto Rican by Esmeralda Santiago

Seeds of America series by Laurie Halse Anderson

Books About Other Life Challenges

I Beat the Odds: From Homelessness, to the Blind Side, and Beyond by Michael Oher

The Outsiders by S.E. Hinton

Freak the Mighty by Rodman Philbrick

Tangerine by Edward Bloor

Chicken Boy by Frances O'Roark Dowell

Joey Pigza series by Jack Gantos

22124208R00038

Printed in Great Britain
by Amazon